Homophones, Synonyms & Antonyms Activity Book

A Reading FUNdamentals™ Book

BARKER CREEK

Homophones, Synonyms & Antonyms

Text and Illustration
Copyright © 2016
by Barker Creek Publishing, Inc.

All rights reserved. No part of this book may be reproduced in any form without permission in writing from Barker Creek Publishing, Inc., P.O. Box 2610, Poulsbo, WA 98370, USA, except by a newspaper or magazine reviewer who wishes to quote brief passages in a review. If you are employed as a school teacher or an institutional worker, you have the publisher's permission to reproduce the lessons in this book to the extent necessary for use in your classroom to accompany your lessons. Purchase of this book does not entitle reproduction of any part of this book for an entire school, district or system. Such use is strictly prohibited.

*Graphic Designer:
Vickie Spurgin*

Printed in the USA

ISBN: 978-1-533003-19-5
Item Number: LL1600

BARKER CREEK®

P.O. Box 2610
Poulsbo, WA 98730
www.barkercreek.com
800.692.5833

Other books in this series include:
Compound Words Activity Book
Nouns Activity Book
Verbs & Adverbs Activity Book
Adjectives Activity Book
Collective Nouns Activity Book
Prefixes/Suffixes Activity Book
Idioms Activity Book
Similes Activity Book

Chart Sets in this series include:
Idioms Chart Set
Grammar Poster Set

All of the titles in our Reading FUNdamentals™ series are also available as E-Books.

Visit us at www.barkercreek.com for more information.

Homophone

a word that sounds the same as another word but has a different meaning

hare • hair
flower • flour
to • two

Synonym

a word that has the same or nearly the same meaning as another word

earth • world
smart • intelligent
dad • father

Antonym

a word that means the opposite of another word

day • night
near • far
start • finish

Table of Contents

How to use this book/Ideas..... 4

Homophones 5
- flour/flower............. 6
- bare/bear................ 7
- male/mail................ 8
- sale/sail................. 9
- night/knight 10
- hare/hair............... 11
- week/weak 12
- blue/blew.............. 13
- write/right 14
- tail/tale................ 15
- fair/fare............... 16

Synonyms 17
- earth/world 18
- doctor/physician....... 19
- couch/sofa............. 20
- bucket/pail............ 21
- dad/father............. 22
- detergent/soap........ 23
- suitcase/luggage 24
- car/automobile........ 25
- chef/cook 26
- present/gift........... 27
- gas/fuel............... 28

Antonyms 29
- infant/adult 30
- empty/full............. 31
- winter/summer........ 32
- sunrise/sunset 33
- miniature/gigantic 34
- near/far............... 35
- top/bottom 36
- start/finish............ 37
- east/west 38
- frozen/melted 39
- tall/short.............. 40

Review Test 41

Templates
- Homophone............ 42
- Synonym............... 43
- Antonym............... 44

Pictures
- Homophone....... 45-46
- Synonym.......... 47-48
- Antonym.......... 49-50

How to Use This Book

Please read through this entire page before getting started.

There are three main sections in this book; *homophones*, *synonyms*, and *antonyms*. Within each section, there are 11 related lessons, all in a similar format. You may choose to use these lessons as an INTRODUCTION of the skill or simply for a REVIEW of the skill.

Page Set Up

1. Set it in concrete!
Say the word, write the word neatly, then spell it WITHOUT looking at the word. Look at the word to check your spelling.

2. Nail it down!
Use the dictionary to define the word.

3. Create a blueprint!
Draw the word.

4. Tack it on!
You may need to use a separate piece of paper for some of these activities. Many are "hands-on" extensions. These can be done in a whole group setting, individually or for homework.

5. Dig in!
Write a sentence using the correct meaning(s) for each word(s).

Review Test

Measure what your students have learned. See the test on page 41.

Answer Key

HOMOPHONE	SYNONYM	ANTONYM
1. week	1. pail - bucket	1. adult
2. right	2. luggage - suitcase	2. melted
3. mail	3. doctor - physician	3. miniature
4. tail	4. car - automobile	4. near
5. knight	5. cook - chef	5. finish
	6. fuel - gas	6. frozen
	7. dad - father	7. summer

Blank Page Templates

Templates for each type of word (*homophone*, *synonym*, and *antonym*) are provided on pages 42-44. Use these templates to create activity pages for words of your choice.

Picture Cards

There are 55 related REPRODUCIBLE pictures on pages 45-50 to supplement the lessons.

Here are some ideas for using the pictures:

- **Flash cards**
  After every lesson, give each student the related picture to color and glue onto an index card. Keep in library pockets or small bags for flash card games.

- **Riddles**
  Have the students make up riddles and allow the class to answer the riddles by holding up the correct picture card.

- **Creative Stories**
  Provide students with five to ten various pictures to incorporate in a creative writing lesson. The story could be in rebus form where pictures are used in place of words.

- **Alphabetical order**
  Put the pictures in ABC order.

- **Mini books**
  Put the picture cards in a book format to take home and enjoy.

- **Go Fish!**
  Make **four** of the *homophones*, *synonyms* and *antonyms* pictures. Using cardstock, print four copies of the homophones pictures. Cut into individual cards and store in a library pocket or small bag when not in use. Repeat with the synonyms and antonyms pictures to create additional GO FISH games. Great for a center activity!

What is a homophone?

a word that sounds the same as another word but has a different spelling and meaning

Reading FUNdamentals™ Homophones

Name: _____

flour • flower

Set in concrete!
Say it! Write it! Spell it!

Say it!	Write it!	Spell it! (Don't look!)
flour		
flower		

Nail it down!
Define it! What does it mean? Look it up in the dictionary.

flour _____
_____

flower _____
_____

Create a blueprint!
Draw it!

flour	flower

Tack it on!
Extend it!

Make sugar cookies from scratch. Using cookie cutters, cut them into flower shapes. Bake, decorate, and enjoy. YUM! YUM!

Dig in!
Use it!

Write each word in a sentence.

1. **flour**: _____

2. **flower**: _____

Reading FUNdamentals™
Homophones

Name: _____

bare • bear

Set in concrete!
Say it! Write it! Spell it!

Say it!	Write it!	Spell it! (Don't look!)
bare		
bear		

Nail it down!
Define it!
What does it mean? Look it up in the dictionary.

bare _____
_____

bear _____
_____

Create a blueprint!
Draw it!

Tack it on!
Extend it!

On a large piece of paper, create a barefoot bear. Paint the bottoms of your feet and place them on the paper (heels together and feet separated about three inches). Let dry. The toes serve as ears. Add the face, eyes, nose and mouth using markers.

Dig in!
Use it!

Write each word in a sentence.

1. **bare**: _____

2. **bear**: _____

Reading FUNdamentals™ Homophones

Name: _____

male • mail

Set in concrete!
Say it! Write it! Spell it!

Say it!	Write it!	Spell it! (Don't look!)
male		
mail		

Nail it down!
Define it!
What does it mean? Look it up in the dictionary.

male _____
_____

mail _____
_____

Create a blueprint!
Draw it!

male	mail

Tack it on!
Extend it!

Write a short letter to a male member of your family. This could be your dad, brother, grandpa, uncle or cousin. Place the letter in an envelope, address, and send. Be sure to add a stamp!

Dig in!
Use it!

Write each word in a sentence.

1. **male:** _____

2. **mail:** _____

Reading FUNdamentals™
Homophones

Name: _____

sale • sail

Set in concrete!

Say it! Write it! Spell it!

Say it!	Write it!	Spell it! (Don't look!)
sale		
sail		

Nail it down!

Define it!
What does it mean? Look it up in the dictionary.

sale _____
_____

sail _____
_____

Create a blueprint!

Draw it!

Tack it on!

Extend it!

Design a small sailboat using various scrap items such as fabric, straws, plastic tubs, etc. Next, write an advertisement for the newspaper with the caption, "*Check out this sailboat! It's on SALE!*"

Dig in!

Use it!

Write each word in a sentence.

1. **sale**: _____

2. **sail**: _____

Reading FUNdamentals™ — Homophones, Synonyms & Antonyms ©2016 www.barkercreek.com

Reading FUNdamentals™ Homophones

Name: _____

night • knight

Set in concrete!
Say it! Write it! Spell it!

	Say it!	Write it!	Spell it! (Don't look!)
	night		
	knight		

Nail it down!
Define it!
What does it mean? Look it up in the dictionary.

night _____
_____

knight _____
_____

Create a blueprint!
Draw it!

night	knight

Tack it on!
Extend it!

Write a short story containing three to five paragraphs about a knight who does funny things at night. Be creative!

Dig in!
Use it!

Write each word in a sentence.

1. **night**: _____

2. **knight**: _____

Reading FUNdamentals™
Homophones

Name: _____

hare • hair

Set in concrete!
Say it! Write it! Spell it!

Say it!	Write it!	Spell it! (Don't look!)
hare		
hair		

Nail it down!
Define it!
What does it mean? Look it up in the dictionary.

hare _____
_____

hair _____
_____

Create a blueprint!
Draw it!

hare	hair

Tack it on!
Extend it!

Look through some magazines and find a picture of a person. Cut out his or her hair. Glue this "wig" onto a separate piece of paper and add a hare's face and body. Do not forget his long, floppy ears!

Dig in!
Use it!

Write each word in a sentence.

1. **hare**: _____

2. **hair**: _____

Reading FUNdamentals™ Homophones

Name: _____

week • weak

Set in concrete!
Say it! Write it! Spell it!

Say it!	Write it!	Spell it! (Don't look!)
week		
weak		

Nail it down!
Define it!
What does it mean? Look it up in the dictionary.

week _____
_____
weak _____
_____

Create a blueprint!
Draw it!

week	weak

Tack it on!
Extend it!

On a separate piece of paper, list the days of the week. Next to each day, write five VERBS describing activities that you could DO that day. Be sure each verb begins with the beginning letter for that particular day of the week. *(Example: Monday-march)* After this week, you will not be weak, you will be strong!

Dig in!
Use it!

Write each word in a sentence.

1. **week**: _____

2. **weak**: _____

Reading FUNdamentals™
Homophones

Name: _____

blue • blew

Set in concrete!
Say it! Write it! Spell it!

Say it!	Write it!	Spell it! (Don't look!)
blue		
blew		

Nail it down!
Define it!
What does it mean? Look it up in the dictionary.

blue _____
_____

blew _____
_____

Create a blueprint!
Draw it!

blue	blew

Tack it on!
Extend it!

Illustrate this sentence: **The blue kite blew in the wind.**

Dig in!
Use it!

Write each word in a sentence.

1. **blue**: _____

2. **blew**: _____

Reading FUNdamentals™ — Homophones, Synonyms & Antonyms ©2016 www.barkercreek.com

Reading FUNdamentals™ Homophones

Name: _____

write • right

Set in concrete!

Say it! Write it! Spell it!

Say it!	Write it!	Spell it! (Don't look!)
write		
right		

Nail it down!

Define it! What does it mean? Look it up in the dictionary.

write _____
_____

right _____
_____

Create a blueprint!

Draw it!

write	right

Tack it on!
Extend it!

Try to write your name using *your toes* on your *right foot*. Good luck!

Dig in!

Use it!

Write each word in a sentence.

1. **write**: _____

2. **right**: _____

Reading FUNdamentals™
Homophones

Name: _____

tail • tale

Set in concrete!
Say it! Write it! Spell it!

Say it!	Write it!	Spell it! (Don't look!)
tail		
tale		

Nail it down!
Define it!
What does it mean? Look it up in the dictionary.

tail _____
_____

tale _____
_____

Create a blueprint!
Draw it!

tail	tale

Tack it on!
Extend it!

Write a tale about " **The Famous Fish Tail**."

Dig in!
Use it!

Write each word in a sentence.

1. **tail**: _____

2. **tale**: _____

Reading FUNdamentals™ — Homophones, Synonyms & Antonyms ©2016 www.barkercreek.com

Reading FUNdamentals™ Homophones

Name: _____

Set in concrete!

Say it! Write it! Spell it!

Say it!	Write it!	Spell it! (Don't look!)
fair		
fare		

Nail it down!

Define it! What does it mean? Look it up in the dictionary.

fair _____
_____

fare _____
_____

Create a blueprint!

Draw it!

fair	fare

Tack it on!

Extend it!

Pretend you are at the fair. The fare for each ride is 50 cents. If you go on two rides, how much would that cost? Five rides? Eight rides? Eleven rides? Show your work on a separate piece of paper.

Dig in!

Use it!

Write each word in a sentence.

1. **fair**: _____

2. **fare**: _____

What is a synonym?

a word that has the same or nearly the same meaning as another word

Reading FUNdamentals™ Synonyms

Name: _____

earth • world

Set in concrete!
Say it! Write it! Spell it!

Say it!	Write it!	Spell it! (Don't look!)
earth		
world		

Nail it down!
Define it!
What does it mean? Look it up in the dictionary.

earth/world

_____

_____

Create a blueprint!
Draw it!

earth/world

Tack it on!
Extend it!

Locate the United States on a map or globe. What countries are on the other side of the world? Name at least three.

Dig in!
Use it!

Write each word in a sentence.

1. **earth:** _____

2. **world:** _____

18   Reading FUNdamentals™ — Homophones, Synonyms & Antonyms ©2016 www.barkercreek.com

Reading FUNdamentals™ Synonyms

Name: _____

doctor • physician

Set in concrete!

Say it! Write it! Spell it!

Say it!	Write it!	Spell it! (Don't look!)
doctor		
physician		

Nail it down!

Define it!

What does it mean? Look it up in the dictionary.

doctor/physician

_____

_____

Create a blueprint!

Draw it!

doctor/physician

Tack it on!

Extend it!

Abbreviations are shortened forms of words. What is the abbreviation for **doctor**?

Dig in!

Use it!

Write each word in a sentence.

1. **doctor**: _____

2. **physician**: _____

Reading FUNdamentals™
Synonyms

Name: _____

couch • sofa

Set in concrete!
Say it! Write it! Spell it!

Say it!	Write it!	Spell it! (Don't look!)
couch		
sofa		

Nail it down!
Define it!
What does it mean? Look it up in the dictionary.

couch/sofa

_____

_____

Create a blueprint!
Draw it!

couch/sofa

Tack it on!
Extend it!

Draw your favorite place to sit and relax. What makes this place so special? Write a paragraph describing this place.

Dig in!
Use it!

Write each word in a sentence.

1. **couch**: _____

2. **sofa**: _____

Reading FUNdamentals™ Synonyms

Name: _____

bucket • pail

Set in concrete!
Say it! Write it! Spell it!

Say it!	Write it!	Spell it! (Don't look!)
bucket		
pail		

Nail it down!
Define it!
What does it mean? Look it up in the dictionary.

bucket/pail

_____

_____

Create a blueprint!

Draw it!

bucket/pail

Tack it on!

Extend it!

Illustrate this poem:
Jack and Jill went up the hill to fetch a pail of water.
Jack fell down and broke his crown, and Jill came tumbling after.

Dig in!

Use it!

Write each word in a sentence.

1. **bucket**: _____

2. **pail**: _____

Reading FUNdamentals™ Synonyms

Name: _____

dad • father

Set in concrete!

Say it! Write it! Spell it!

Say it!	Write it!	Spell it! (Don't look!)
dad		
father		

Nail it down!

Define it!
What does it mean? Look it up in the dictionary.

dad/father
_____
_____

Create a blueprint!

Draw it!

dad/father

Tack it on!

Extend it!

Brainstorm other synonyms for dad or father with a few friends.

Dig in!

Use it!

Write each word in a sentence.

1. **dad:** _____

2. **father:** _____

Reading FUNdamentals™ Synonyms

Name: _____

detergent • soap

Set in concrete!
Say it! Write it! Spell it!

Say it!	Write it!	Spell it! (Don't look!)
detergent		
soap		

Nail it down!
Define it!
What does it mean? Look it up in the dictionary.

detergent/soap

_____

_____

Create a blueprint!
Draw it!

detergent/soap

Tack it on!
Extend it!

Do you remember to wash your hands before you eat? To ensure that you wash thoroughly, while you are lathering, sing the *Happy Birthday* song. Keep washing until you sing the *entire* song. Now that's clean!

Dig in!
Use it!

Write each word in a sentence.

1. **detergent**: _____

2. **soap**: _____

Reading FUNdamentals™ — Homophones, Synonyms & Antonyms ©2016 www.barkercreek.com

Reading FUNdamentals™ Synonyms

Name: _____

suitcase • luggage

Set in concrete!
Say it! Write it! Spell it!

Say it!	Write it!	Spell it! (Don't look!)
suitcase		
luggage		

Nail it down!
Define it!
What does it mean? Look it up in the dictionary.

suitcase/luggage

_____
_____

Create a blueprint!
Draw it!

suitcase/luggage

Tack it on!
Extend it!

If you were going to take a trip to the moon and could take only 10 items, what would they be? List these on a separate piece of paper.

Dig in!
Use it!

Write each word in a sentence.

1. **suitcase**: _____

2. **luggage**: _____

Reading FUNdamentals™ Synonyms Name: _____

Set in concrete!

Say it! Write it! Spell it!

Say it!	Write it!	Spell it! (Don't look!)
car		
automobile		

Nail it down!

Define it!
What does it mean? Look it up in the dictionary.

car/automobile

_____

Create a blueprint!

Draw it!

car/automobile

Tack it on!

Extend it!

Draw a picture of a car. Label its parts.

Dig in!

Use it!

Write each word in a sentence.

1. **car**: _____

1. **automobile**: _____

Reading FUNdamentals™ — Homophones, Synonyms & Antonyms ©2016 www.barkercreek.com

Reading FUNdamentals™ Synonyms

Name: _____

chef • cook

Set in concrete!
Say it! Write it! Spell it!

Say it!	Write it!	Spell it! (Don't look!)
chef		
cook		

Nail it down! Define it!
What does it mean? Look it up in the dictionary.

chef/cook
_____
_____

Create a blueprint! Draw it!

chef/cook

Tack it on! Extend it!
Imagine that you are a chef at a very fancy restaurant. What would definitely be on the menu? List at least five choices and write a description for each as you would want them to appear in your menu.

Dig in! Use it!
Write each word in a sentence.

1. **chef**: _____

2. **cook**: _____

26   Reading FUNdamentals™ — Homophones, Synonyms & Antonyms ©2016 www.barkercreek.com

Reading FUNdamentals™ Synonyms

Name: _____

present • gift

Set in concrete!

Say it! Write it! Spell it!

Say it!	Write it!	Spell it! (Don't look!)
present		
gift		

Nail it down!

Define it!
What does it mean? Look it up in the dictionary.

present/gift

_____

_____

Create a blueprint!

Draw it!

present/gift

Tack it on!
Extend it!

Pretend you have wrapped a present in a box and no one knows what it is. Provide five very helpful clues to tell a partner. Can he/she guess what is in the box? You may have to give more clues.

Dig in!

Use it!

Write each word in a sentence.

1. **present**: _____

2. **gift**: _____

Reading FUNdamentals™ Synonyms

Name: _____

gas • fuel

Set in concrete!

Say it! Write it! Spell it!

Say it!	Write it!	Spell it! (Don't look!)
gas		
fuel		

Nail it down!

Define it!
What does it mean? Look it up in the dictionary.

gas/fuel
_____
_____

Create a blueprint!

Draw it!

gas/fuel

Tack it on!

Extend it!

Assume your family's car holds 20 gallons of gas. How much money would it take to fill up the car's tank if the gas was $1.50 per gallon? $1.80 per gallon? $2.00 per gallon?

Dig in!

Use it!

Write each word in a sentence.

1. **gas**: _____

2. **fuel**: _____

28   Reading FUNdamentals™ — Homophones, Synonyms & Antonyms ©2016 www.barkercreek.com

What is an antonym?

a word that means the opposite of another word

Reading FUNdamentals™ Antonyms

Name: _____

infant • adult

Set in concrete!
Say it! Write it! Spell it!

Say it!	Write it!	Spell it! (Don't look!)
infant		
adult		

Nail it down!
Define it!
What does it mean? Look it up in the dictionary.

infant _____
_____

adult _____
_____

Create a blueprint!
Draw it!

infant	adult

Tack it on!
Extend it!

Using a magazine, cut out a picture of an infant. Do the same for an adult. Compare each one. How are they alike? How are they different?

Dig in!
Use it!

Write each word in a sentence.

1. **infant**: _____

2. **adult**: _____

Reading FUNdamentals™ Antonyms

empty • full

Set in concrete!
Say it! Write it! Spell it!

Say it!	Write it!	Spell it! (Don't look!)
empty		
full		

Nail it down!
Define it!
What does it mean? Look it up in the dictionary.

empty _____

_____

full _____

_____

Create a blueprint!
Draw it!

empty | full

Tack it on!
Extend it!

Pour water into a container. Now empty it into a measuring cup to see how much the container holds.

Dig in!
Use it!

Write each word in a sentence.

1. **empty**: _____

2. **full**: _____

Reading FUNdamentals™ — Homophones, Synonyms & Antonyms ©2016 www.barkercreek.com

Reading FUNdamentals™ Antonyms

Name: _____

winter • summer

Set in concrete!
Say it! Write it! Spell it!

Say it!	Write it!	Spell it! (Don't look!)
winter		
summer		

Nail it down!
Define it!
What does it mean? Look it up in the dictionary.

winter _____

summer _____

Create a blueprint!
Draw it!

winter	summer

Tack it on!
Extend it!

List all of the winter and summer holidays. Which holiday is your favorite? Why?

Dig in!
Use it!

Write each word in a sentence.

1. **winter**: _____

2. **summer**: _____

32   Reading FUNdamentals™ — Homophones, Synonyms & Antonyms ©2016 www.barkercreek.com

Reading FUNdamentals™
Antonyms

Name: _____

sunrise • sunset

Set in concrete!

Say it! Write it! Spell it!

	Say it!	Write it!	Spell it! (Don't look!)
	sunrise		
	sunset		

Nail it down! Define it!
What does it mean? Look it up in the dictionary.

sunrise _____
_____

sunset _____
_____

Create a blueprint! Draw it!

sunrise	sunset

Tack it on! Extend it!

The sun rises in the _____ and sets in the _____.

Dig in! Use it!

Write each word in a sentence.

1. **sunrise**: _____

2. **sunset**: _____

Reading FUNdamentals™ — Homophones, Synonyms & Antonyms ©2016 www.barkercreek.com

Reading FUNdamentals™ Antonyms

Name: _____

miniature • gigantic

Set in concrete!

Say it! Write it! Spell it!

Say it!	Write it!	Spell it! (Don't look!)
miniature		
gigantic		

Nail it down!

Define it!
What does it mean? Look it up in the dictionary.

miniature _____
_____

gigantic _____
_____

Create a blueprint!

Draw it!

miniature	gigantic

Tack it on!

Extend it!

Draw a miniature elephant and a gigantic flea. Write a creative story about them.

Dig in!

Use it!

Write each word in a sentence.

1. **miniature**: _____

2. **gigantic**: _____

Reading FUNdamentals™ Antonyms

Name: _____

near • far

Set in concrete!
Say it! Write it! Spell it!

Say it!	Write it!	Spell it! (Don't look!)
near		
far		

Nail it down!
Define it!
What does it mean? Look it up in the dictionary.

near _____
_____
far _____
_____

Create a blueprint!
Draw it!

near	far

Tack it on!
Extend it!

What relative lives nearest to you?
What relative lives the farthest away from you?

Dig in!
Use it!

Write each word in a sentence.

1. **near**: _____

2. **far**: _____

Reading FUNdamentals™ Antonyms

Name: _____

top • bottom

Set in concrete!
Say it! Write it! Spell it!

Say it!	Write it!	Spell it! (Don't look!)
top		
bottom		

Nail it down!
Define it!
What does it mean? Look it up in the dictionary.

top _____
_____
bottom _____
_____

Create a blueprint!
Draw it!

Tack it on!
Extend it!

Choose an object to describe in great detail from TOP to BOTTOM. Write this in paragraph form.

Dig in!
Use it!

Write each word in a sentence.

1. **top**: _____

2. **bottom**: _____

Reading FUNdamentals™ Antonyms

Name: _____

start • finish

Set in concrete!
Say it! Write it! Spell it!

Say it!	Write it!	Spell it! (Don't look!)
start		
finish		

Nail it down!
Define it! What does it mean? Look it up in the dictionary.

start _____
_____

finish _____
_____

Create a blueprint!
Draw it!

start	finish

Tack it on!
Extend it!

How long does it take you to write the alphabet from START to FINISH (A-Z)? If it was under one minute, try writing it from FINISH to START (Z-A) this time. Which took longer?

Dig in!
Use it!

Write each word in a sentence.

1. **start**: _____

2. **finish**: _____

Reading FUNdamentals™ — Homophones, Synonyms & Antonyms ©2016 www.barkercreek.com

Reading FUNdamentals™ Antonyms

Name: _____

east • west

Set in concrete!
Say it! Write it! Spell it!

Say it!	Write it!	Spell it! (Don't look!)
east		
west		

Nail it down!
Define it!
What does it mean? Look it up in the dictionary.

east _____
_____

west _____
_____

Create a blueprint!
Draw it!

Tack it on!
Extend it!

Find your state on a map.
What is to the EAST of your state? What is to the WEST?

Dig in!
Use it!

Write each word in a sentence.

1. **east**: _____

2. **west**: _____

Reading FUNdamentals™ Antonyms   Name: _____

Set in concrete!

Say it! Write it! Spell it!

Say it!	Write it!	Spell it! (Don't look!)
frozen		
melted		

Nail it down!

Define it!
What does it mean? Look it up in the dictionary.

frozen _____
_____

melted _____
_____

Create a blueprint!

Draw it!

Tack it on!
Extend it!

Fold a piece of blue paper in half. On one side, paint a snowman. On the other side, paint a large sun and the snowman. What does this snowman look like? What happened?

Dig in!

Use it!

Write each word in a sentence.

1. **frozen**: _____

2. **melted**: _____

Reading FUNdamentals™ — Homophones, Synonyms & Antonyms ©2016 www.barkercreek.com

Reading FUNdamentals™ Antonyms

Name: _____

tall • short

Set in concrete!
Say it! Write it! Spell it!

Say it!	Write it!	Spell it! (Don't look!)
tall		
short		

Nail it down!
Define it!
What does it mean? Look it up in the dictionary.

tall _____
_____

short _____
_____

Create a blueprint!
Draw it!

tall	short

Tack it on!
Extend it!

Illustrate a progression of an object going from TALL to SHORT. Use at least five different sizes for the same character.

Dig in!
Use it!

Write each word in a sentence.

1. **tall**: _____

2. **short**: _____

Review Test

Name:

Homophones
Use the correct word in each sentence. Write it in the blank.

1. A _____ contains seven days.
         week   weak

2. Make a _____ turn onto the next street.
         write   right

3. The _____ was not delivered yesterday. It was a holiday.
         male   mail

4. The rabbit's _____ was very soft and furry.
         tail   tale

5. Princess Lily was saved by the brave _____.
         night   knight

Synonyms
Match the word to the left with its synonym on the ht.

1. pail	suitcase
2. luggage	physician
3. doctor	chef
4. automobile	bucket
5. cook	car
6. fuel	father
7. dad	gas

Antonyms
What is the antonym for each word listed below? Write it in the blank.

1. infant _____
2. frozen _____
3. gigantic _____
4. far _____
5. start _____
6. melted _____
7. winter _____

Reading FUNdamentals™
Homophones

Name: _____

Set in concrete!
Say it! Write it! Spell it!

Say it!	Write it!	Spell it! (Don't look!)

Nail it down!
Define it!
What does it mean? Look it up in the dictionary.

Create a blueprint!
Draw it!

Tack it on!
Extend it!

Dig in!
Use it!

Write each word in a sentence.

1. _____

2. _____

42   Reading FUNdamentals™ — Homophones, Synonyms & Antonyms ©2016 www.barkercreek.com

Reading FUNdamentals™
Synonyms

Name: _____

Set in concrete!
Say it! Write it! Spell it!

Say it!	Write it!	Spell it! (Don't look!)

Nail it down!
Define it!
What does it mean? Look it up in the dictionary.

_____
_____
_____
_____

Create a blueprint!
Draw it!

Tack it on!
Extend it!

_____
_____

Dig in!
Use it!

Write each word in a sentence.

1. _____ _____

2. _____ _____

Reading FUNdamentals™ — Homophones, Synonyms & Antonyms ©2016 www.barkercreek.com

Reading FUNdamentals™
Antonyms

Name: _____

Set in concrete!
Say it! Write it! Spell it!

Say it!	Write it!	Spell it! (Don't look!)

Nail it down!
Define it!
What does it mean? Look it up in the dictionary.

Create a blueprint!
Draw it!

Tack it on!
Extend it!

Dig in!
Use it!

Write each word in a sentence.

1. _____

2. _____

44   Reading FUNdamentals™ — Homophones, Synonyms & Antonyms ©2016 www.barkercreek.com

HOMOPHONE PICTURES

HOMOPHONE PICTURES

SYNONYM PICTURES

SYNONYM PICTURES

ANTONYM PICTURES

ANTONYM PICTURES